HEARTSTRINGS

Patrice McMullen

BookLeaf Publishing

India | USA | UK

Presentation by BookLeaf Publishing

Web: www.bookleafpub.com

E-mail: info@bookleafpub.com

ISBN: 9789358360660

First edition 2021

PREFACE

I was given the opportunity to participate in a writing challenge which is how you are reading this little book of poetry. This writing challenge was just that, as it was during a difficult period in my life. I hope these poems speak to you in some way shape or form and tug on your heartstrings, even a little bit.

DEDICATIONS

Dad, for patting my head, packing away the hard stuff when I couldn't, and being patient with me.

Mum, for reminding me there's always another way and that this too shall pass. As Rosie said, I'd be lost without you.

Claire, for giving me the music, movies and literature that would soothe my soul and put my heart back together again every time.

Aaron, for being in my corner for the whole fight and after it, and for reminding me of my worth even when I don't believe it.

Joce, for keeping me here when I didn't want to be anymore. For telling me how it is, but more importantly how it will be if I keep…moving…forward.

ACKNOWLEDGMENT

Thank you to BookLeaf Publishing for being given the opportunity to bring to light my voice and my heart. Thank you to my parents and siblings for nourishing, strengthening and repairing my heartstrings my whole life. Thank you to my family on both sides, for encouraging me to be myself always. Thank you to my oldest friends and my newest friends for being patient and kind with my heart after you picked it off the floor, dusted it off, and held it in your hands to keep it safe for a while. To Bek, thank you for a photograph of me that makes me feel beautiful and Ben for encouraging me to smile. To my mum, thank you for the inspiration for the book cover, and Jocelyn for trying to get there. To those I didn't get to say thank you to, you know who you are, here's to you as well.

Thank you to those who tugged at my heartstrings in order to write these poems.

Design Credit:

Cover - Canva

Photograph – Rebekah Brindle

Sometimes

my old insecurities

come out to play

when I least expect

and I have to remind myself

it is different,

it is better,

they didn't leave

because of me,

they left because of

them.

-        insecurity

I gave you my heart

And you have me a smile

Said you still loved me

But this was it for a while

I gave you my heart

And you have me a smile.

I gave you my heart

And you have me a cross

Said it would replace

All the things my heart lost

I gave you my heart

and you gave me a cross.

I gave you my heart

And you gave me goodbye

Said you liked what we started

But you just couldn't lie

I gave you my heart

And you gave me goodbye

I gave you my heart

And you gave me a butterfly

Said someone always falls

But it wasn't you this time

I gave you my heart

And you gave me a butterfly.

-      I gave you my heart

Do you get everything handed to you on a silver platter?

You act as if it doesn't even matter.

The chances you get given are so often and many,

the appeal was lost when the count hit twenty,

the boy next door who caught the big break,

I can't wait for the world to realise you're fake,

you were everything and the whole world didn't matter,

Then you got everything handed to you on a silver platter.

And my head, my heart, my body, it shattered.

But no worry, no need, no matter-

for you had everything handed to you on a silver platter.

-      silver platter

Thank you for giving me

painting videos, even though

I can't watch them anymore.

Thank you for giving me

obscure funny videos, even though

I don't laugh at them anymore.

Thank you for giving me

horror movies, even though

I can't watch them with anyone else.

Thank you for giving me

you, even though

I can't have you anymore.

-    phthalo blue

I promise if you just

give me some more time

I'll be able to figure out

the right words

to make you stay.

-       you could stay?

I guess I figured

after all this time

I was worth more

than an unread

message.

-	I guess I figured

Are you gonna be the one

to fill the hole in my heart?

I bet that you aren't,

I bet that you aren't.

-        the bet

You were almost mine,

I think that's the worst kind,

I think that's the worst kind of love.

You were almost mine to hold,

I guess I should've known,

I guess I should've known better.

You were almost mine to keep,

now I just can't sleep,

now I just can't sleep at all.

You were almost mine forever,

I should've known better,

I should've known better about you.

\-   you were almost mine

I'll wait for you always

because there's

no one else's laugh

I want to hear

intersected with mine,

or anyone else's snores

to keep me awake at night,

or anyone else's lips

to kiss my forehead.

   -     even if I wait forever

For the calm reserved quiet

you feel at the edge of day.

For the sweet whisper in the night

that asks if you'll stay.

For the long hard goodbye

that pleads you not to go,

so why did you go?

Why did you go?

- the question

I could fit in your

pocket and not

make a sound.

You could carry me,

till you were ready

to get me back out.

You could do everything

you needed to do

and I would still be there

I would wait

in your pocket

even if you forgot.

-    pocket

I wish there hasn't been

a knock that interrupted,

telling you to leave.

I would've stayed in

your embrace forever,

even just a minute more.

What I would give

for a minute more

with you.

        -     just a minute more

I thought after you

told me you loved me

it would take more than

two weeks for you to

swipe right on your

new home.

-       hypocrite

It was the place I found my soul,

the place I wept for days,

the place my heart expanded,

the place I wish I stayed.

It was the place we laughed for hours,

the place we made our own,

the place we sometimes hated,

the place we called our home.

It was the place that held hard times,

and the place it held the best,

the place I know I took for granted,

the place I won't forget.

It was the place we fought about nothing,

and you couldn't predict the weather,

the last place we have to remember,

what it was like sharing a room together.

I wish our beach would take us,

and send us out to sea,

so we didn't have to move on,

from the place meant for you and me.

- 	daisy street

Thank you for letting me forget about him

even if it was just for a night,

thank you for talking for hours

sending my heartbreak just out of sight.

Thank you for making me forget

that my heart had broken in two,

for letting me live out a moment

where I wished it was me and you.

Thank you for letting me realise,

that the sun comes out from the clouds,

but also for making me remember

what was lost it too can be found.

Thank you for getting my hopes up

and bringing them back down again,

for reminding me I have to heal first

but for giving me a new friend.

-      the new friend

I gave you my heart

and you gave me a hug,

said I would wait and you

met my eyes with a shrug.

I gave you my heart

and you gave me a hug.

I gave you my heart

and you gave me I love you,

said you had work to do

and you hoped I would too.

I gave you my heart

and you gave me I love you.

-    I gave you my heart again

The sound of you keeps me

from falling back down,

the look you give me stops

my immense fear of this town,

the feel of you on my chest

keeps me from going insane,

your scent on my clothes clears

the dark thoughts in my brain,

the touch of you on my skin

heals my heart from the pain,

but your name in my throat

keeps me from crying again.

    -    O and M

The thought of opening up

my body to someone again

makes me sob uncontrollably,

because why would I want to

share a piece of my skin

when they won't know it

the way you did.

-    I thought you felt the same

Keep looking at the stars kid,

they might get a little dimmer.

Keep looking at the grass kid,

it might get a little thinner.

Keep looking at the trees kid,

they might get a little smaller.

Keep looking at the world kid,

even when you get a little taller.

Keep laughing at the world kid,

it might get a little meaner.

Keep playing dawn till dusk kid,

before the days go a little quicker.

Keep running at top speed kid,

the air might get a little thicker.

Keep playing in the dirt kid,

It might get a little sicker.

Keep dreaming of big things kid,

it'll make the world a little better.

    -    L

I tied a piece of my heart

to your heart,

so you'd always know where to find it.

I tied a knot so tight

no one else,

could untie it.

I tied a piece of my soul

to your soul,

so you'd always know where to find it.

I tied a piece of my heart

to your heart,

so one day maybe…

you will find it.

- heartstrings